Inside
Government

ELECTING THE
PRESIDENT

Barbara Silberdick Feinberg

Twenty-First Century Books

A Division of Henry Holt and Company

New York

Twenty-First Century Books
A Division of Henry Holt and Company, Inc.
115 West 18th Street
New York, NY 10011

Henry Holt® and colophon are trademarks of
Henry Holt and Company, Inc.
Publishers since 1866

Published in Canada by Fitzhenry & Whiteside Ltd.
195 Allstate Parkway, Markham, Ontario L3R 4T8

Library of Congress Cataloging-in-Publication Data

Feinberg, Barbara Silberdick.
Electing the president / Barbara Silberdick Feinberg. — 1st ed.
p. cm. — (Inside government)
Summary: Discusses the presidential election process including primaries,
nominations, national conventions, campaigns, and the electoral college.
Includes bibliographical references and index.
1. Presidents—United States—Election—Juvenile literature.
[1. Presidents—Election.] I. Title. II. Series.
JK524.F45   1995
324.6'3'0973—dc20   94–41763
                                                        CIP
                                                        AC

ISBN 0-8050-3422-6
First Edition—1995

Designed by Kelly Soong

Printed in Mexico
All first editions printed on acid-free paper ∞.
10 9 8 7 6 5 4 3 2 1

Photo Credits

Cover: Flag image courtesy of U.S. Government Printing Office, Mt. Rushmore
© Frank LaBua/Gamma-Liaison

p. 8, 19, 38: UPI/Bettmann; p. 11, 31: The Bettmann Archive; p. 13, 18, 29:
UPI/Bettmann Newsphotos; p. 16, 26, 46: North Wind Picture Archives; p. 21: Joe
Traver/The Gamma Liaison Network; p. 23, 33, 41, 49: AP/Wide World Photos; p.
42: J.L. Atlan/Sygma.

☆

To my aunt Ethel Steinberg Scheldon, a woman of courage, independence, intelligence, and compassion

☆ ══════ ACKNOWLEDGMENTS ══════ ☆

I would like to thank the following people and institutions for helping me locate some of the information used in this book: the Federal Election Commission; Jeremy R. Feinberg, Columbia University School of Law, Class of 1995; Suzanne Freedman, freelance researcher; staff members of the Republican and Democratic National Committees; and Lisa Olivieri, Senior Information Service Assistant, ABC News.

I am also grateful to the following people who encouraged me while I was preparing the manuscript: Doug and Jeremy Feinberg, Gina Cane, Naomi Neft, Lillian Williams, Paula Ruderman, Jeanie Smart, and Susan Zito. They endured my grumbles and moans at times when I had put in too many hours at the word processor and shared my joy when I found an interesting fact to present to my readers.

☆ *April 1994*

CONTENTS

ONE
CELEBRATING A PRESIDENTIAL ELECTION

Every four years, Americans celebrate the election of their president with pomp and ceremony. The president's inauguration, when he takes the oath of office, is a gala occasion. The actual swearing-in ceremony is, however, a serious and dignified event. Starting with George Washington, all presidents of the United States have promised to "faithfully execute the office of President of the United States" and to "preserve, protect, and defend the Constitution of the United States." The Constitution is a set of basic rules that describes and limits the powers of the national government. George Washington added the phrase "So help me God" and swore upon a Bible. The presidents who came after him did not always follow his example. But, since James Buchanan became president in 1857, almost all presidents have taken their oath with a hand on the Bible.

Starting with Thomas Jefferson in 1801, most presidents have been inaugurated in Washington, D.C. Earlier presidents (George Washington and John Adams) took their oaths of office in New York City and Philadelphia, each city having served as the nation's Capital. Deaths and assassinations have caused a number of presidents to be sworn in at unexpected places. In 1923, when President Warren Harding died, Vice President Calvin Coolidge took his presidential oath in his father's Vermont farmhouse by the light of a kerosene lamp. Forty years later, Vice President Lyndon B. Johnson was sworn in on board *Air Force One,* the presidential plane, upon the assassination of President John F. Kennedy.

☆ ══════ ☆

President Lyndon B. Johnson, flanked by his wife, Ladybird, and Jacqueline Kennedy, was sworn in by District Judge Sarah T. Hughes of Dallas before returning to Washington, D.C.

Originally, the new president was sworn in on March 4. In 1933, the date was shifted to January 20 by the Twentieth Amendment. Amendments make changes in the Constitution's rules and procedures. Since new presidents and members of Congress, the nation's lawmakers, are elected in November, the amendment shortened the time defeated or retiring officials may stay in office.

Balls, parades, and receptions have become part of the national inaugural celebration. The first inaugural ball was held by James Madison in 1809. Now, presidents dance with their partners at as many as nine of these festivities. The number of balls has increased to allow thousands of presidential friends, supporters, and admirers to attend.

Madison also began the practice of having military troops

march in his parade. The parades took place on the way to the inauguration. Since President Benjamin Harrison took office in 1889, however, parades have been held after the swearing-in ceremony. Unlike the presidents who came before him, Harrison chose to watch the parade instead of marching in it. Usually, the outgoing president has escorted the incoming president to the inauguration. In 1801, though, John Adams felt so bitter about Thomas Jefferson's victory that he refused to attend. Similar feelings also kept John Quincy Adams in 1829, Martin Van Buren in 1841, and Andrew Johnson in 1869 from taking part in the festivities with their successors.

In 1829, Andrew Jackson became the first president to invite the public to a reception at the White House after he was sworn in. He greeted unruly mobs who damaged the White House furniture in a hunt for souvenirs. Not all presidents have followed his example. In 1992, however, ordinary citizens were invited to line up and shake hands with President Bill Clinton in the White House after his inauguration. They were orderly and well behaved.

The inauguration marks the end of a long and often exhausting struggle to win an election. It also marks the beginning of four years of difficult responsibilities. The president of the United States is the most powerful elected official in the nation. Subject to approval by Congress, he appoints federal judges, ambassadors to foreign nations, heads of government departments, and directors of other government organizations. He may decide to send the armed services to fight in wars. The president makes sure that existing laws are carried out and informs the lawmakers about conditions in the nation. The chief executive, as the president is sometimes known, also makes suggestions for new laws because Americans expect their presidents to provide leadership in solving national problems. In addition, the president decides how the United States will deal with other nations and often negotiates treaties with them. He is responsible for keeping the nation safe and secure from its enemies.

These are just some of the most important presidential duties listed in the Constitution.

Presidents also have other demands on their time. Quite often, they serve as the chief spokesperson for their political party. Political parties sponsor candidates for public office and help them get elected. Presidents have often made public appearances and speeches to help members of their party get elected. They also represent the nation at public ceremonies. For example, on Memorial Day, they might lay wreaths at the Tomb of the Unknown Soldier in Arlington National Cemetery. In 1910, President William H. Taft threw out the first baseball of the season, starting a happier presidential custom. Presidents are also expected to entertain the leaders of other nations who visit the United States.

Presidents may only serve for two terms of office, or eight years. The two-term tradition was started by George Washington and continued until Franklin D. Roosevelt. President Roosevelt was first elected in 1932 and was reelected in 1936, 1940, and 1944. He had first won office during the Great Depression, when the nation's economy collapsed, and remained president during most of World War II. The Twenty-second Amendment was passed in 1951 to prevent the voters from repeatedly reelecting a popular president to office even in times of crisis. The amendment put a two-term limit on presidents.

For taking on the responsibilities of office, modern presidents receive a yearly salary of $200,000 from the government. They must pay taxes on it. They also are given $50,000 a year for expenses resulting from their official duties. In addition, they may spend up to $100,000 a year for travel and $20,000 for official entertaining. These sums are not taxable. Presidents do not pay rent to live in the White House, and Congress often gives them money to redecorate the family living quarters. They may relax at the presidential retreat, Camp David, in Maryland. President Dwight D. Eisenhower named the retreat for his grandson. Presidents may also choose to cruise on the presiden-

☆ ═══════ ☆

President William H. Taft tossed the first baseball
of the season on June 9, 1910.

tial yacht. President Harry S. Truman enjoyed playing poker on
board the *Williamsburgh.* Modern presidents receive protection
from the Secret Service even after they leave office. This practice
began after the assassination of President John F. Kennedy in
1963. Retired presidents also receive pensions from the government and free secretarial help.

Americans look for certain qualities in their presidents. The
Constitution sets only three conditions. A president must have
been born in the United States, must be at least thirty-five years
old, and must have lived in the United States for at least fourteen
years. At age forty-three, John F. Kennedy was the youngest man
elected president; and at forty-two, Theodore Roosevelt was the
youngest to be sworn in as president, having been vice president
when President William McKinley was assassinated. The nation's
oldest president was Ronald W. Reagan, who was seventy-three
when he was reelected in 1984.

The public has set other conditions for holding office, but these have changed over time. Until the election of John F. Kennedy in 1960, Americans refused to accept a Catholic as president. They feared that a Catholic political leader would have to divide his loyalty between the needs of the nation and the demands of his religion. The public was also reluctant to have a divorced person as president before Ronald W. Reagan was elected in 1980. He had remarried long before he was elected. Earlier, it was felt that a divorced person could not be a moral leader of the nation.

The major political parties have not yet picked a woman to run for president. In 1984, however, the Democrats selected Geraldine Ferraro as their vice presidential candidate. Throughout most of American history, women were treated as the weaker sex, unsuited for political life. African-Americans have not been welcomed as presidential candidates either, but Jesse Jackson weakened the racial barrier. In 1988, he finished second in a field of eight Democratic candidates trying to become the party's choice for president.

In the early years of the American republic, it seemed as if Americans preferred presidents who were born in Virginia, because four of the first five presidents were natives of that state. Four other presidents were also born in Virginia. Seven presidents, however, have come from Ohio, and four each from Massachusetts and New York. Fifteen other states have contributed presidents to the nation. (See chart in appendix.)

Americans usually want their presidential candidates to have served in public life. That way, the voters can judge their record of achievements. Sixteen presidents have been governors, with valuable experience in running their states. (See chart in appendix.) Thirty-two have served in Congress, where they became familiar with the workings of the national government. (See chart in appendix.) Six were military heroes. They were successful leaders in times of difficulty even if they had little political experience. (See chart in appendix.) Some candidates

☆ ══════ ☆

Geraldine Ferraro became the first woman
to be a vice presidential candidate.

have been dark horses, men whose names the public did not recognize. In 1976, people teased candidate Jimmy Carter by calling him "Jimmy Who?" Carter campaigned all around the country until Americans grew quite familiar with his name and even voted him into office.

American citizens are privileged to be able to vote for their president. Voting, however, is just one part of the long and complicated process of electing a president. Choosing the most qualified person to hold the nation's highest office involves nominations, campaigning, funding, and a two-stage election. The way Americans pick their presidents has changed over time and has occasionally brought unexpected results. This is what makes the study of presidential elections so fascinating.

TWO
GETTING NOMINATED

During the first twelve years of government under the Constitution, no presidential candidates were nominated to compete for election. Individuals in each state, chosen by the people or appointed by state lawmakers, simply elected the president as the Constitution required. These individuals, known as electors, were expected to vote for the most capable men in the nation. Whoever won more than 50 percent of their votes became president, and the runner-up served as vice president. This is how George Washington and John Adams were chosen.

Nominations of competing candidates for president developed only with the rise of political parties. (See chart in appendix.) At first, the parties were made up solely of politicians. They developed the earliest method of nominating would-be presidents, the caucus. Caucuses were meetings of the members of Congress from the same political party to choose a candidate for president. The first official nominating caucus was held in February 1804 when more than 100 Democratic-Republican congressmen came together in Washington, D.C. They selected Thomas Jefferson as their presidential candidate. He had almost completed his first term in office. They also picked Governor George Clinton of New York for his vice president.

The caucus system fell apart in 1824 when most of the Democratic-Republican members of Congress failed to show up to nominate a presidential candidate. The congressmen who were present chose William Harris Crawford of Georgia as their candidate. Four other presidential hopefuls—Andrew

Jackson, Henry Clay, John Quincy Adams, and John C. Calhoun—refused to be bound by their decision. They got state lawmakers and mass meetings of voters and politicians to nominate them. By 1828, nominating caucuses no longer met. Instead, the rival candidates, President John Quincy Adams and Senator Andrew Jackson of Tennessee, were picked by state lawmakers and voters.

By 1831, most white male adults had gained the right to vote. The political parties of the day, the Democrats and the National Republicans, could no longer survive if they limited their membership to professional politicians. So they began to recruit members from the public. At this point, the parties organized mass meetings of voters and politicians and held the first national party conventions. These eventually became large-scale gatherings of delegates, representing party members from each state. They agreed to meet every four years, the summer before the November election, to choose presidential and vice presidential candidates.

In the past, professional party politicians controlled the nominations. They held brokered conventions, at which they met in private and agreed on a candidate. Then they engineered his victory by instructing their state delegations to vote for the candidate. They also made deals to get other state delegations to support their choice. This is how Mark Hanna, an Ohio political leader, got the Republican National Convention to nominate William McKinley for president in 1896 and 1900. In later years, Democratic presidential candidates Woodrow Wilson and Franklin D. Roosevelt were also the choices of brokered conventions.

The Democrats found a way to help professional politicians conduct brokered conventions. They required that candidates be chosen by the unit rule. Delegates from each state had to cast all their votes for the candidate favored by a majority of the state's delegates. Usually, state political leaders decided which candidate a majority of their delegates would support. This lim-

☆ ═══ ☆

Climax of the Republican National Convention
held in Chicago when James G. Blaine was defeated
for the nomination by William McKinley.

ited participation by ordinary delegates in the candidate selection process and gave control of the convention to professional politicians. In 1968, the Democrats eliminated the unit rule. The Republicans never used it.

Traditionally, state party organizations have chosen delegates to the national convention. The delegates voted at conventions the way their leaders wanted. For generations, this system excluded women, young people, and minorities. In the 1960s, these previously neglected groups became more active in politics. In 1968, their protests against the Vietnam War and racial discrimination and their demands to be heard by the delegates disrupted the Democratic National Convention in Chicago. As a result, both parties quickly reformed the way delegates were selected, to better reflect the diversity of the American people.

Today, within each state, delegates are usually chosen by a combination of three methods. Party members in local districts meet, or hold caucuses, to pick delegates to a state convention, who in turn elect the state's delegation to the national convention. Alternatively, local party organizations hold formal elections to choose representatives to state party conventions at which delegates to the national conventions are selected. In other states, members of the party vote directly for state delegates pledged to specific presidential candidates.

Elections to choose delegates or even the candidates themselves are called primaries. They were intended to encourage ordinary party members to take part in the nominations process and to weaken the control of the professional politicians over the party conventions. Florida introduced the presidential primary in 1901, followed by Wisconsin in 1905. By 1924, primaries were held in seventeen states, but they became less popular during the 1920s and 1930s. Voters and candidates lost interest, and the contests were thought to be too costly to continue. In 1948, interest in primaries revived when Republican presidential hopeful Harold E. Stassen, former governor of Minnesota, almost won the nomination by running in primaries. He had an unbroken string of victories until he lost the major primaries in Oregon and New York. Those defeats destroyed his chances.

Primaries soon became an important measure of a candidate's popularity in different regions of the country. For example, Senator John F. Kennedy's victory in the West Virginia primary in 1960 showed that voters would accept a Catholic candidate. Primaries still did not automatically guarantee the nomination. In 1968, Senators Eugene J. McCarthy of Minnesota and Robert F. Kennedy of New York (who was assassinated prior to the convention) had won many primaries, but Vice President Hubert Humphrey became the Democratic presidential candidate. He had not entered a single primary race but had the support of many important state party leaders. Today, presidential hopefuls must enter primaries to win their party's nomination.

Senator John F. Kennedy on his barnstorming tour stops
to shake hands with steel workers in Huntington, West Virginia.

Most primaries are scheduled between March and June of
a presidential election year. Would-be candidates usually start
campaigning two years earlier. They face an exhausting schedule
and mounting expenses. Early contests, such as the New
Hampshire primary, are used to decide which candidates look
most promising. They receive a lot of media attention. All but
two Republican candidates quit after their poor showing in
New Hampshire in 1980. In 1984, five Democratic candidates
dropped out of the race for the nomination for the same reason.
It has been suggested that a national primary day be set up so
that party members in all states have an equal chance to select
from a wide field of candidates. On March 10, 1992, Democratic
primaries were held in eight states, mostly in the South, as well
as three caucuses. Because so many contests were held on that
one day, it was called Super Tuesday. As yet, neither party has
agreed to a national primary day.

State primary laws often pledge delegates to specific candidates. They are required to vote for those candidates at the national convention. Some delegates may be bound to a particular candidate only for the first ballot or for later ballots. As a result, victories in the primaries offer presidential hopefuls a chance to win enough delegates to capture the party's nomination before the convention meets. This reduces the possibility of having a brokered convention.

Today, national party conventions are noisy, cheerful events with banners, streamers, balloons, and posters displaying the names of the presidential hopefuls. They seem like huge sports events, packed with cheering people supporting their favorite players. Instead of watching athletes perform, however, the delegates listen to a great number of speeches. For example, on the first day of the convention, they hear the keynote address, intended to whip up enthusiasm for the party. Many more speeches will follow in the days to come. Despite all the festivities, the delegates manage to accomplish a lot of work. They approve the party's platform, giving the party's stand on

☆ ═══════ ☆

Representative Barbara Jordan from Texas waves
to the audience after delivering the keynote speech
at the Democratic National Convention in 1976.

the political issues of the day. They may also vote on changes in the party's rules. These are prepared by committees of party members.

Attendance at national conventions has changed over time. At first, the number of representatives each state sent to the Democratic and Republican conventions was based on its population. States where the most people lived were entitled to the most delegates. At the turn of the century, only 1,000 or so delegates attended the party conventions. Beginning in 1916, the Republican Party gave bonus delegates to states according to the number of votes Republican candidates received in previous elections. In 1944, the Democrats awarded bonus delegates to states that the party had won in the last presidential election. In 1984, the Democrats appointed party and government officials as super delegates. This was intended to restore some of the power professional politicians had lost as a result of the primaries. There were 4,313 Democratic delegates and 2,206 Republican delegates at the 1992 national conventions.

In 1952, millions of Americans were able to watch the national conventions on television from beginning to end. In 1980, given the rising costs of coverage and dwindling audiences, the major networks no longer covered the entire proceedings. By that time, the conventions were less suspenseful. As more primaries were being held throughout the nation, most Americans pretty much knew who each party's candidates would be. Some specialized public affairs stations, however, still continued the lengthy broadcasts.

The main business of the convention is the nomination of presidential and vice presidential candidates. This generally occurs on the third day. Meanwhile, the candidates keep in touch with their teams of assistants, who work to keep delegates contented and loyal. In the past, favorite son nominations took up a lot of time. State delegations often proposed their governors or other popular state officials for president to honor or reward them for outstanding service to the state. This is why

☆ ═══════ ☆

*The final night at the Democratic National Convention
in 1992 was filled with banners and balloons.*

Governor Robert Meyner of New Jersey was nominated at the
1960 Democratic convention and the name of the governor of
California, Ronald W. Reagan, was placed on the ballot at the
1968 Republican convention. Usually, favorite son candidates
did not have enough support outside their states to win the
party's nomination. In 1972, the Democratic Party ended these
nominations by requiring that every candidate supply the names
of at least fifty delegates from three or more states who have
pledged their support.

Speeches are given to officially nominate the party's competing candidates for president. In the past, these speeches were
short. In 1860, it took only twenty-seven words to place
Abraham Lincoln's name in nomination. Since then, nominating speeches have grown longer and more elaborate, despite the
time requirements of television networks. In 1988, Governor
Bill Clinton of Arkansas was allowed fifteen minutes to talk

about Governor Michael Dukakis of Massachusetts. He spoke for more than half an hour.

After each nominating speech, the candidate's delegates wave posters and banners to demonstrate their support. Short seconding speeches come next. Films may celebrate the major candidates' careers, highlighting their achievements. In 1992, Democratic delegates could watch important moments in Bill Clinton's life projected on a huge movie screen. Republicans were treated to a film featuring George H. W. Bush's accomplishments as president.

Once the nomination ceremonies are completed, the secretary of the convention opens the voting with a roll call of states. Usually, the states vote in alphabetical order, but in 1972, the Democrats used a lottery to determine the order of states. This gave each state an equal chance to cast the deciding vote that would give victory to one of the nominees. The chairperson of each state delegation announces how many votes from that state are to be given to the candidate. (Some states allow delegations to split their vote.)

Republican candidates are chosen by a simple majority vote of the delegates, one-half the total number of delegates plus one. For many years, Democratic nominees were selected by two-thirds of the Democratic convention delegates. Since a two-thirds majority was difficult to obtain, it could take a long time and many ballots before presidential candidates were selected. In 1912, Governor Woodrow Wilson of New Jersey became his party's official candidate on the 46th ballot; and in 1924, William G. McAdoo, a former secretary of the treasury, won on the 103d ballot. These lengthy sessions were quite an ordeal for the delegates because the conventions met during the summer months and air-conditioning was not yet invented. The 1936 Democratic convention finally abolished the two-thirds rule in favor of a simple majority.

Since Dwight D. Eisenhower won the Republican Party's nomination in 1952, the candidates of both parties have been

☆ ═══════ ☆

Franklin D. Roosevelt walked to the stage
to deliver his acceptance speech, despite the
heavy braces on his legs.

chosen on the first ballot. Once a presidential candidate has won, there is an acceptance speech. This tradition started with Franklin D. Roosevelt, who spoke at the Democratic National Convention in 1932. He wanted to show the delegates that he was energetic and active despite having been crippled by polio.

Once the presidential nominee is picked, the convention must select a vice presidential candidate. In the past, party leaders made the choice without necessarily consulting the presidential nominee. In 1940, however, Franklin D. Roosevelt forced the Democrats to accept his secretary of agriculture, Henry A. Wallace, for the post by threatening not to run. Nowadays, the conventions routinely approve their presidential candidate's choice. Nevertheless, there are speeches and then a formal vote.

Geography often influences the selection of a presidential running mate. The party wants to "balance the ticket" by having candidates from different parts of the country to appeal to different sets of voters. For this reason, in 1968, Republican candidate Richard M. Nixon of California chose Spiro T. Agnew of Maryland to run with him. In 1992, Democratic candidate Bill Clinton of Arkansas ignored this practice and selected Albert Gore from the neighboring state of Tennessee. Once the vice presidential candidate is chosen, the convention comes to an end.

Now it is time to campaign. Campaigning is the way candidates appeal to voters. It gives the public a chance to judge the way candidates conduct themselves under pressure. It offers the nominees the opportunity to better understand what Americans want and need from their leaders.

THREE
CAMPAIGNING FOR VOTES

Political campaigns are appeals to the public to vote for a certain candidate or all the candidates of a certain party. Such appeals became increasingly important once more Americans gained the right to vote. Until the 1830s, under most state laws, only white men who owned property were permitted to vote. Propertyless men were thought to lack the proper background to vote intelligently. By the early 1830s, as more people moved west and settled on their own land, property restrictions on voting were ended.

The voting public, or the electorate, continued to expand. After the Civil War, the Fifteenth Amendment (1870) to the Constitution gave African-American men the right to vote, but it took a number of national civil rights voting laws in the late 1950s and in the 1960s before they could really exercise that right in many places. Women were finally permitted to vote in all states when the Nineteenth Amendment (1920) was approved. The Twenty-third Amendment (1961) gave people who lived in the District of Columbia the opportunity to take part in presidential elections. The Twenty-sixth Amendment (1971) let eighteen-, nineteen-, and twenty-year-olds participate in elections.

Modern-day presidential candidates have to appeal to a greater number of different voters; they also have farther to travel. As the United States expanded from thirteen original states to fifty, presidential candidates had to seek votes over larger distances. Over time, primaries opened up nominations to ordinary voters. As a result, presidential hopefuls had to compete in more elections.

The votes candidates need are not evenly distributed. Some states have larger populations, and therefore more voters, than others. Party strength is not evenly divided among the states either. Republicans tend to be more successful in midwestern and western states. Democrats do better in northeastern industrial states. Until the 1980s, the South was solidly Democratic. More people identify with the Democratic Party than the Republican Party, but they do not necessarily vote.

In the past, presidential candidates felt that it was undignified for them to appeal for votes. Instead, they stayed home and relied on professional politicians to rally support for them. Republican candidate Benjamin Harrison conducted one such front-porch campaign. He simply greeted visitors who came to see him at his home in Indianapolis. This practice has continued into modern times in a slightly different form. Presidents seeking reelection often remain in the White House, looking and acting like dignified heads of state. They are using the "Rose Garden" strategy, named for the White House Rose

☆ ═══════ ☆

General Benjamin Harrison seems very calm as he
receives the election results by dispatches in his library at home.

Garden, outside the Oval Office where presidents work. For example, in 1992, President George H. W. Bush often let others campaign for him while he stayed in Washington, D.C., to govern the nation.

In 1860, Democrat Stephen A. Douglas was the first presidential candidate to make personal appearances around the nation. On the eve of the Civil War, he tried unsuccessfully to get pro-slavery and anti-slavery Democrats in the North and South to cooperate. No other candidate followed his example until 1896, when Democratic candidate William Jennings Bryan traveled more than 18,000 miles and gave over 600 speeches. By the 1930s, all presidential candidates were expected to tour the nation.

Traditionally, presidential campaigns have begun in September, after Labor Day. Recently, some candidates have wanted an earlier start. Ronald W. Reagan gave a number of campaign speeches in August. As they plan their campaigns, candidates must decide where to appear, how to present themselves, and what to say. It is difficult for them to develop their strategy, or plan of action. There are no guarantees that a particular approach will work. Despite candidates' best efforts, the outcome of an election can depend on events beyond their control. In 1932, Republican candidate Herbert C. Hoover was defeated, in large part, by the Great Depression, which brought the nation's economy to a standstill. It did not help Jimmy Carter's reelection chances in 1980 that the government of Iran refused to release the Americans it held hostage.

Presidential nominees have had to choose between visiting all fifty states or limiting themselves to states with large voting populations and/or states they are favored to win. Republican candidate Richard M. Nixon pledged to visit every state in his 1960 campaign. His opponent, Democrat John F. Kennedy, took the opposite approach and won the election. Similarly, presidential hopefuls have had to decide whether to enter all primaries or just the ones they are more certain of winning. In 1976, Jimmy Carter ran everywhere and gained enough delegates to become the Democratic presidential candidate. In 1988, Albert Gore lost the Democratic presidential nomination because he concentrated his efforts on primaries in the South, where he was better known. His opponents won primaries in other states on the same day and canceled out the effect of his regional victory.

Candidates have traveled around the country by train, plane, and bus in search of votes. In 1948, Harry S. Truman took train trips across the United States in a whistle-stop campaign, visiting towns so small that the stationmaster had to blow a whistle to get trains to stop there. In 1992, Bill Clinton briefly revived the whistle-stop campaign, but he toured small towns by bus, rather than by train. Clinton, like other modern candidates, traveled mostly by plane so that he could visit more states in less time.

Television has forced candidates to make other decisions about campaign appearances. In both primary and presidential campaigns, they are often given the chance to debate one another. Televised debates began in 1960 with presidential candidates Richard M. Nixon and John F. Kennedy. Nixon lost the debates partly because of the way he appeared on camera and not because of the things he said. Others have suffered by comparison with their opponents on television. In a 1976 debate with Jimmy Carter, President Gerald R. Ford got his facts about Eastern Europe wrong. During the 1980 New Hampshire primary, a bitter dispute took place between two leading Republican presidential hopefuls, George H. W. Bush and Ronald W. Reagan. Bush offered to debate Reagan but refused to appear onstage with the other candidates Reagan brought with him. Reagan seemed to be the champion of fair play at Bush's expense. Bush had not wanted to share publicity with these less well-known competitors. A debate was finally held between the two men without television coverage. During a debate with George H. W. Bush in 1988, Michael Dukakis failed

☆ ══════ ☆

Presidential nominees, Senator John F. Kennedy (left) and
Vice President Nixon, just before appearing on
their first television debate in September 1960.

to show sufficient emotion. Television viewers seem more interested in the candidates' personality and appearance than in the
positions they take. Ronald W. Reagan was a poor debater, but
he did well in the 1980 debates because the viewers found him
relaxed and charming.

During the 1992 primaries and presidential campaigns,
some of the candidates relied on radio and television call-in
shows to reach voters. Modern technology allowed them to
speak directly with people all over the nation. These were called
"town meetings" because they reminded Americans of New
England town meetings in which ordinary citizens discuss problems and vote on local laws. The 1992 presidential candidates
preferred the call-in shows to television news interview shows.
Reporters on those shows tended to question them more close-
ly than the public did. Whether future candidates continue to

prefer call-in shows to interview shows remains to be seen. Whether candidates replace personal tours of the nation with call-in shows also awaits the future.

How candidates present themselves to the voters requires other decisions. Some claim to be political outsiders. They criticize national politics and promise to do things differently. Relative political unknowns, such as Jimmy Carter and Bill Clinton, have won by emphasizing that they are not part of the Washington scene. Obviously, presidents seeking reelection cannot claim to be outsiders. They must run on their record and let the voters judge how well they performed. Fourteen presidents have been returned to office. Yet, in 1976, Gerald R. Ford lost his bid for reelection. So did George H. W. Bush in 1992. What worked in one election does not necessarily work in another.

Nominees give much thought to what they will say to the voters. Some nominees, such as Republican Barry Goldwater in 1964 and Democrat George McGovern in 1972, stressed a definite and narrow set of ideas. Their extreme positions offended voters within their own party as well as independent voters they sought to attract. Their successful opponents, Lyndon B. Johnson (1964) and Richard M. Nixon (1972), appealed to the common views more voters held. Some candidates, like Democrat Walter Mondale in 1984, told voters how he felt about a number of issues that divided the country. He lost the election to Ronald W. Reagan, who spoke in generalities. In 1992, Democrat Bill Clinton talked about his specific solutions to national problems and won.

Candidates have to decide how they will deal with their opponents. In recent years, they have been criticized for negative campaigning, releasing unflattering or potentially damaging information about their rivals. In 1988, ads for Republican George H. W. Bush repeatedly mentioned that Democrat Michael Dukakis, as governor of Massachusetts, had let Willie Horton, a hardened criminal, join a weekend prison-release program. The ad suggested that the governor was soft on crime.

Negative campaigning, however, is not new. In a vicious campaign before the election of 1800, Thomas Jefferson was accused of being a coward during the American Revolution, cheating a widow out of her inheritance, and other character flaws. Nevertheless, he was victorious. During the 1884 presidential campaign, Democratic candidate Grover Cleveland was accused of fathering a baby and failing to marry the child's mother. He admitted the charge in public. Despite evidence that his opponent, Republican James G. Blaine, was guilty of personal immorality and political corruption, Cleveland refused to use the information and won the election.

Presidential nominees have always had campaign managers to help them win office. These individuals, often party officials, were especially important in the days when candidates conducted front-porch campaigns. Today, campaign managers

☆ ══════ ☆

A cartoon published in 1884 shows Grover Cleveland being tormented by his illegitimate child.

have just as much, if not more, to do. They help plan strategy and manage a staff of specialists who arrange the candidate's schedule, organize rallies, prepare speeches, collect information, and attend to other important tasks. In 1988, Democrat Michael Dukakis hired Susan Estrich as his campaign manager. She became the first woman to run a presidential campaign for a major political party.

Some specialists working on the candidate's staff conduct polls, questioning people about their opinions of the candidates and issues. Polls have been used since 1824. They have not always been reliable. For example, in 1948, polls falsely predicted that Harry S. Truman would lose the election. Polltakers had stopped asking questions too early in the campaign, and other mistakes were made in the polling. Techniques have since improved. It was after John F. Kennedy's campaign in 1960 that candidates began to hire specialists to run their own polls. Other sophisticated methods are also used now to find out what the public thinks about the candidates. These include focus groups of individuals selected for certain qualities, such as age or income, who talk together about particular topics with a discussion leader.

Modern campaigns make use of media consultants. These specialists plan a candidate's television commercials and other advertising. In 1952, Republican Dwight D. Eisenhower became the first nominee to use a lot of the television spots. Now they are commonplace during campaigns. The specialists try to create a good image of the candidate. They have to handle the disclosure of information that might embarrass the nominee or damage his campaign. In one case, in 1992, they had to cast Bill Clinton's efforts to avoid being drafted to fight in the Vietnam War in a positive light. Some people are concerned that in modern campaigns, the public sees an image created by media specialists rather than the actual candidate.

Among the most important specialists in any presidential campaign are the people who raise money for the candidate and

☆ ═══════ ☆

The Chicago Daily Tribune *published too early on election night in November 1948 with the wrong headline.*

the party. In 1896, financier Mark Hanna collected $16 million for William McKinley's campaign. Modern presidential election expenses have soared even higher. In 1992, Bill Clinton raised $115.2 million; George H. W. Bush, $100.5 million; and H. Ross Perot, $80.9 million. Today, most of the money is spent on television commercials. In 1988, they cost Republican candidate George Bush around $30 million. Other major expenses are polls, travel, and staff.

In the past, "fat cats," or wealthy individuals, contributed most of the campaign funds. Fears that they might have too much influence over the government produced the first campaign finance law in 1907. It was soon followed by others. These laws banned contributions from certain groups, such as federal employees. They also set spending limits and required nominees to report donations and expenses. There was, however, no way to enforce the laws, so parties and candidates usually ignored them.

In 1971, members of Congress tried a new approach, publicly financed presidential campaigns. They passed the Federal Election Campaign Act. It allowed taxpayers to check off on their income tax returns whether they wanted to contribute $1.00 (now $3.00) to the campaigns. Beginning with the 1976 presidential election, the federal government matched the funds the candidates raised, up to $10 million. To qualify, the candidates had to meet certain requirements. National conventions also received federal money. Later, these amounts were adjusted for rising costs, and a matching fund program was set up for primaries, too. Still, there was no agency to enforce the laws.

In 1972, Republican Richard M. Nixon ran in the last privately financed presidential election. Afterward, Congress discovered that the heads of a number of major corporations had made large contributions to his campaign. Some of these business leaders were told to donate the money if they wanted favorable treatment from the government. Others gave because they were threatened with unfavorable government action, such as investigations into their tax payments to the government. Nixon supporters also collected illegal contributions. These were deposited in foreign banks and then brought back to the United States so that they would be harder to trace.

As a result of their investigation of Nixon's campaign finances, members of Congress passed another series of reforms in 1974. Since then, these laws have been changed and improved. They set further limits on spending and fund-raising, both for primaries and the presidential election. Candidates were required to give more detailed information about campaign contributions and expenses. Now, individuals may donate only $1,000 to each primary and general election campaign, up to a total of $25,000 for all national candidates and $20,000 for committees of national parties.

The 1974 reforms also limited contributions by independent committees known as political action committees (PACs). Political action committees are groups set up by labor, business, and others interested in a particular issue to raise funds for candidates. Candidates have even set up their own PACs. For example, 1986 Democratic presidential hopeful Richard Gephardt's Effective Government Committee helped other Democrats campaign. Most of the $1 million it raised, however, paid for Gephardt's travel expenses to the presidential primaries and for his campaign workers. At this time, PACs may give only $5,000 to each candidate and $15,000 to committees of the national parties. The law does not, however, prevent them from giving money to unregulated state party organizations and some nonparty committees that can help a candidate win an election. Such nonparty committees may conduct drives to educate people about the issues or get out the vote.

In 1974, Congress also set up the Federal Election Commission (FEC) to make sure campaign finance laws were obeyed. Candidates must send the FEC frequent reports, listing specific contributors and primary and election campaign expenses. As a result, a nominee's campaign financing specialists and their staffs not only raise funds but also must fill out numerous forms required by the FEC. To do this, they have to keep accurate records. The FEC has been criticized because it can do little to limit the activities of PACs. These committees have grown in number from 2,551 in 1980 to 4,094 in 1991. Yet, PACs claim their activities fall within their constitutional rights to free speech and freedom to associate. The courts have upheld them.

Campaigning for the presidency is a test of stamina, skill, and strategy. It takes a great deal of planning and costs a vast amount of money. Despite this, every four years, candidates willingiy go through this ordeal to convince the voters to elect them. Some have suggested that presidential campaigns be cut down to a few weeks before the election to save time and money. Others prefer to leave things as they are. Whether or not changes are eventually made, voters will still have to decide which candidate will be victorious.

FOUR
VOTING FOR THE PRESIDENT

Every four years, on the first Tuesday after the first Monday in November, a date set by Congress, Americans vote to choose the president of the United States as the Constitution requires. States have added their own rules about voting, making certain that these do not violate the Constitution or its amendments. Usually, voters are required to live within a state voting district for at least thirty days before an election. States also allow members of political parties to be present at each polling (voting) place to make sure the election is fair.

Voters go to their local polling place and pull levers on a voting machine or mark a paper ballot to indicate their choices. Because they vote in private, Americans are said to have the secret ballot. No one has the right to know how a person voted unless he or she decides to make that information public. The machines automatically record the total vote for each candidate. Paper ballots are counted by hand. If voters are ill, or temporarily living outside their home state, serving in the armed services, or attending college, they may use an absentee ballot. This is a piece of paper listing the candidates for office. It is mailed to voters if they tell election officials in advance that they will be out of the state on Election Day.

Voters generally must choose between the candidates of the two major political parties of the day. Since the 1830s, they have also had the chance to give their support to a candidate from a minor party, or third party, in twenty-three presidential elections. (See chart in appendix.) Voting for third-party candidates allows the public to express its dissatisfaction with the major parties. Typically, these candidates do not have enough nationwide support to win a presidential election. As a result of the 1971 Federal Election Campaign Law, third parties can receive matching funds from the government for their campaigns. They must win at least 5 percent of the vote in the election to qualify. As a result, they usually get federal funds after the election.

There are three types of third parties. One is formed for the purpose of electing a popular leader. For example, the Progressive (Bull Moose) Party was set up to nominate Theodore Roosevelt for president in 1912. Another kind unites people who share a well-defined set of ideas about the way society and government should be run. The Socialist Party offered candidates Eugene V. Debs several times from 1900 and Norman Thomas in 1932 to bring about more equality in American life through a particular economic program. Other parties develop around particular causes or issues. The Prohibition Party, which ran seven candidates for president from the 1880s to 1916, campaigned to get Americans to stop drinking alcoholic beverages. More recently, in 1992, H. Ross Perot formed the United We Stand Party to demand that the government take action to reduce the huge debt it had run up.

Minor parties rarely last for many presidential elections. If they become popular with voters, they are absorbed by one of the major parties. To avoid losing its voters, the major party will adopt the third party's most popular positions on the issues and/or sponsor the same candidate. For example, William Jennings Bryan ran as both a Populist and a Democrat in the elections of 1896 and 1900. He spoke out in favor of reforming the nation's money system, a Populist cause. This helped destroy the Populist Party.

The only third party that became a major party was the Republican Party. In 1860, its candidate, Abraham Lincoln, won the election. On the eve of the Civil War, northern and southern

Democrats could no longer unite behind one candidate, and they split the party's vote. Once Lincoln became president, more people joined the Republican Party. It continued to benefit from the weakened condition of the Democratic Party long after the Civil War ended.

On Election Day, voters may be presented with a number of presidential candidates. They must also choose among other candidates for national, state, and local offices. Popular presidential nominees may help other members of their party win these offices. If voters admire a particular candidate, they are likely to support other candidates from the same party, especially if the candidates have the personal endorsement of the presidential candidate. This is called the coattails effect.

In 1932, Franklin D. Roosevelt's victory brought other Democrats to power. In 1980, Republican candidates benefited from Ronald W. Reagan's election. Not every president is as successful as Roosevelt and Reagan were. For example, a

☆ ══════════ ☆

Ronald W. Reagan campaigning with Senator Paul Laxalt,
a Republican from Nevada.

Democratic majority was elected to Congress at the same time Republican presidents Richard M. Nixon and George H. W. Bush were elected. What's more, even the most popular presidents have been unsuccessful when they campaigned for party members in off-year elections, when presidential elections were not held.

More people vote in presidential elections than in off-year elections. In recent presidential election years, however, only about 50 to 60 percent of the people eligible to vote have actually turned out to do so. From 1840 to 1900, the turnout ranged between 70 and 80 percent. In those days, the electorate was smaller. Only men could take part in elections. Modern studies suggest that better-educated, wealthier, and older Americans are most likely to vote. People who feel strongly about a political party, a candidate, or a particular issue will also tend to turn out for an election. Compared to 100 other nations, though, the United States has been twelfth from the lowest in voter participation.

There are a number of reasons people do not vote. There are Americans who do not care who will become president. It makes no difference to them. Since Election Day is not a holiday for many people, some cannot or will not take time off from their jobs. Others are discouraged from becoming voters because of complicated requirements in some states. The political parties and a number of citizens groups hold drives to encourage nonvoters to participate in elections. Also, many states have made it easier to become a voter.

There have been at least fifteen close presidential elections in American history. If nonvoters had voted, the results might have been different. In 1880, Republican James A. Garfield won 48.27 percent of the popular, or people's, vote, while Democrat Winfield S. Hancock got 48.25 percent. As recently as 1960, Democrat John F. Kennedy received 49.72 percent of the popular vote to Republican Richard M. Nixon's 49.55 percent. This is why every vote counts.

Even if many Americans don't vote in elections, they have always been eager to find out who their next president will be. Newspapers were the only public source of election returns for the first fourteen presidential elections. Then, in 1844, the results were sent by telegraph for the first time. People could learn about Democratic Party candidate James K. Polk's victory over Whig nominee Henry Clay more quickly. In 1920, Pittsburgh radio station KDKA gave the Harding–Cox presidential election results in the nation's first commercial broadcast. Since the 1940s, television has covered the elections.

Now, in the computer age, the television networks can project the winner long before the voting is over. They take exit polls, asking people how they have voted as they leave their polling places. From exit polls in as few as 5 percent of the voting districts in a state, they can predict who will win the state. With information from enough states, they can project a candidate's victory. In 1976, however, the election was so close that NBC did not report that Democrat Jimmy Carter had defeated Republican Gerald R. Ford until 3:30 A.M. EST. On the other hand, in 1980, the networks projected Republican Ronald W. Reagan's victory early in the evening. His opponent, Democrat Jimmy Carter, conceded by 8:50 P.M. EST. Many objected because the announcement was made from the East Coast long before polling places closed on the West Coast.

Because of the three-hour time difference between the East and West Coasts, early projections discourage people living on the West Coast from voting. This could make a difference in the outcome of a close election. Since 1980, the networks have promised not to announce who the probable winner is until people in all the West Coast states have voted. In 1988, CBS did not declare that Republican George H. W. Bush would defeat Democrat Michael Dukakis until 9:17 P.M. In 1992, ABC gave the victory to Democrat Bill Clinton over George Bush at 10:47 P.M.

A number of presidents have won in landslide elections,

President Jimmy Carter concedes early defeat as
he addresses a group of supporters in Washington, D.C.

gaining a very large percentage of the popular vote. Fourteen
successful candidates received 55 percent or more of the vote.
Of these, only four presidents, all elected in the twentieth century, got 60 percent or more of the popular vote. Most presidents
have won between 40 and 50 percent of the vote. When more
than two well-known candidates competed in an election, the
percentages were sometimes lower. For this reason, Abraham
Lincoln was elected president in 1860 with only 39.8 percent of
the popular vote.

    Whether victory is by a large percentage or a small one,
the winning candidate is happy. On election night, a celebration
is held at campaign headquarters. The candidate thanks campaign workers and voters. If he has never been president before,
he soon sets to work with a team of assistants. They make plans

★ ═══════ ★

President-elect George Bush with his family celebrating his victory at Republican National Headquarters in Houston, Texas.

for the time when he takes office. They also start recruiting the people who will be appointed to serve in the government.

By this time, most Americans believe that the election is over. The people have voted, the popular vote has been totaled, and the results announced. They often forget that the results are not yet official. By voting, they have participated in only the first part of a two-stage election. The next stage of the election process has yet to begin.

FIVE

ELECTING A PRESIDENT

Americans vote for president, but they do not actually elect the president. In 1787, the authors of the Constitution felt that people were not wise enough to judge the candidates' qualifications to become president. They also rejected a suggestion to have Congress appoint the president. They feared it would make him too dependent on the lawmakers and too weak to act on his own. Instead, they came up with a plan to let electors choose the president. This is how George Washington and John Adams were elected. (See chapter 2.) Collectively, the electors from all the states are known as the Electoral College. It is still their duty to officially elect the president. Put simply, people elect the electors and the electors elect the president.

The Constitution let the states decide how the electors would be chosen. At first, they were appointed by lawmakers in some states and elected by qualified male citizens in other states. Gradually, political parties in each state started to pick people to serve as their presidential candidate's electors. At the same time, elections began to determine which party's set of electors would actually perform the constitutional duty of voting for the president. Now, in more than half the states, the names of the electors are not even listed on the ballot. Voters think they are directly choosing the president. Actually, they are still selecting electors to make that choice for them. They are voting for the president indirectly.

In about one-third of the states, laws require electors to cast their votes, known as electoral votes, for the candidate who won the vote of the people on Election Day. In other states, the electors are not pledged, but they are expected to vote according to the state's election results. Yet, the unexpected can happen. In 1960, fifteen unpledged electors and an elector who was legally committed to another candidate voted for Senator Harry Byrd of Virginia. Byrd wasn't even an official presidential candidate. This problem could be solved by eliminating the use of human electors and by letting each state's number of electoral votes be counted automatically.

The Constitution outlines the method for calculating how many electoral votes a state may have. It equals the number of lawmakers the state sends to Congress. The number of electoral votes to be distributed among the states is now fixed at 538 because the states have a total of 435 members in the House of Representatives and 100 senators. Three extra electoral votes have been added by the Twenty-third Amendment (1961) to let people living in the District of Columbia vote for the president.

Every ten years, adjustments are made in the number of electoral votes each state receives according to its population growth or decline. First, the United States government conducts a census. It counts how many people there are in the nation and where they are living. Based on this population count, electoral votes are redistributed among the states. So are seats in the House of Representatives, which is also based on population. For example, after the 1990 census, fewer people were found to be living in New York. As a result, the state's electoral votes were reduced by three, as were the number of representatives it sent to Congress. Because more people had moved to Texas, it gained three more electoral votes and three seats in the House.

States with the largest populations have the most electoral votes. They have more influence over presidential elections than the other states. In 1888, Democratic candidate President Grover Cleveland received 48.6 percent of the popular vote, and his Republican rival, Benjamin Harrison, had 47.8 percent. Still, Harrison became president. He had 233 electoral votes to Cleveland's 168. This happened because Harrison won New York. That state had enough electoral votes to give him the victory. If Cleveland had won in New York, he might have been reelected. In fact, he was reelected four years later and became the only president to serve for two terms that did not follow each other.

Elections of this kind have led some people to suggest that the Electoral College be eliminated. They would let voters elect the president directly. That way, the winner of the popular vote would certainly become president. The president would still be chosen by areas where the most people live. States with small populations, however, would be hurt by this plan. They have at least three electors apiece now. Without these guaranteed electoral votes, they would have little influence over the election. In addition, taking away electoral votes could further weaken the part the states play in the American system of government.

In each state, the winning candidate is awarded all the electoral votes. In a very close election, the almost victorious runner-up does not get any electoral votes. Some people think this winner-take-all system is unfair. It does not accurately reflect the way people voted in a state. Overall, it distorts the popular vote, sometimes with strange results. In 1912, Woodrow Wilson was the top vote-getter in forty states. He was elected president with 81.9 percent of the electoral vote but only 41.8 percent of the popular vote. The system also discourages the growth of minor parties. Despite the total number of popular votes these parties receive, they do not gain many electoral votes because they rarely win the popular vote within a state. In 1968, for instance, George C. Wallace's American Independent Party earned 13.5 percent of the popular vote, but the vote was scattered among a number of different states. Wallace won in just five states. For this reason, Wallace ended up with only 8.5 percent of the electoral vote,

The senators and reprefentatives beforementioned, and the members of the feveral ſtate legiſt. latures, and all executive and judicial officers, both of the United States and of the feveral States, ſhall be bound by oath or affirmation, to fupport this conſtitution; but no religious teſt ſhall ever be required as a qualification to any office or public truſt under the United States.

VII.

The ratification of the conventions of nine States, ſhall be fufficient for the eſtabliſhment of this conſtitution between the States fo ratifying the fame.

Done in Convention, by the unanimous confent of the

States preſent, the feventeenth day of September, in the year of our Lord one thouſand feven hundred and eighty-feven, and of the Independence of the United States of America the twelfth. In witneſs whereof we have hereunto fubſcribed our Names.

GEORGE WASHINGTON, Prefident,
And Deputy from VIRGINIA.

NEW-HAMPSHIRE.	John Langdon, Nicholas Gilman.		George Read, Gunning Bedford, Junior, John Dickinſon, Richard Baſſett, Jacob Broom.
MASSACHUSETTS.	Nathaniel Gorham, Rufus King.	DELAWARE.	
CONNECTICUT	William Samuel Johnſon, Roger Sherman.		James M'Henry, Daniel of St. Tho Jenifer, Daniel Carral.
NEW-YORK.	Alexander Hamilton.	MARYLAND.	
NEW-JERSEY.	William Livingſton, David Brearley, William Paterſon, Jonathan Dayton.	VIRGINIA.	John Blair, James Madiſon, Junior.
PENNSYLVANIA.	Benjamin Franklin, Thomas Miſſlin, Robert Morris, George Clymer, Thomas Firzſimons, Jared Ingerſoll, James Wilſon, Gouverneur Morris.	NORTH-CAROLINA	William Blount, Richard Dobbs Spaight, Hugh Williamſon.
		SOUTH-CAROLINA.	John Rutledge, Charles CotesworthPinckney Charles Pinckney, Pierce Butler.
		GEORGIA.	William Few, Abraham Baldwin.

Atteſt, William Jackſon, SECRETARY.

IN CONVENTION, Monday September 17th, 1787.
PRESENT
The States of New-Hampſhire, Maſſachuſetts, Connecticut, Mr. Hamilton from New-York, New-Jerſey, Pennſylvania, Delaware, Maryland, Virginia, North-Carolina, South-Carolina and Georgia:

RESOLVED,

THAT the preceding Conſtitution be laid before the United States in Congreſs aſſembled, and that it is the opinion of this Convention, that it ſhould afterwards be ſubmitted to a Convention of Delegates, choſen in each State by the People thereof, under the recommendation of its Legiſlature, for their aſſent and ratification; and that each Convention aſſenting to, and ratifying the ſame, ſhould give Notice thereof to the United States in Congreſs aſſembled.

Reſolved, That it is the opinion of this Convention, that as ſoon as the Conventions of nine States ſhall have ratified this Conſtitution, the United States in Congreſs aſſembled ſhould fix a day on which Electors ſhould be appointed by the States which ſhall have ratified the ſame, and a day on which the Electors ſhould aſſemble to vote for the Preſident, and the time and place for commencing proceedings under this Conſtitution. That after ſuch publication the Electors ſhould be appointed, and the Senators and Repreſentatives elected: That the Electors ſhould meet on the day fixed for the Election of the Preſident, and ſhould tranſmit their votes certified, ſigned, ſealed and directed, as the Conſtitution requires, to the Secretary of the United States in Congreſs aſſembled, that the Senators and Repreſentatives ſhould convene at the time and place aſſigned; that the Senators ſhould appoint a Preſident of the Senate, for the ſole purpoſe of receiving, opening and counting the votes for Preſident; and, that after he ſhall be choſen, the Congreſs, together with the Preſident, ſhould, without delay, proceed to execute this Conſtitution.

By the unanimous Order of the Convention,
GEORGE WASHINGTON, Prefident.
William Jackſon, Secretary

By order of the Constitutional Convention,
the Electoral College was set up in 1787.

or forty-six votes. Usually, minor parties get between 1 and 3 percent of the popular vote.

In 1992, the *New York Times* reported that Florida voters were thinking about eliminating the winner-take-all system. Instead, they might adopt a proportional system, dividing the state's twenty-five electoral votes among the candidates according to their share of the popular vote. Maine and Nebraska, unlike the other forty-eight states, already use this system. It remains to be seen whether Florida and other states will change the way they distribute electoral votes.

Originally, the Constitution provided that a candidate had to receive a majority of the electoral votes to become president. If no candidate received a majority, or if the candidates were tied, the House of Representatives chose the president from the top five candidates. The first runner-up became vice president. Each state had one vote, and a majority of states was needed for victory. The development of political parties made this arrangement unworkable. During the presidential election of 1800, Democrat-Republican Thomas Jefferson and Aaron Burr each received seventy-three electoral votes. Democratic-Republican electors had wanted Jefferson to become president and Burr to be vice president. When they split their votes between the two candidates, they forgot to arrange to cast fewer votes for Burr. The House of Representatives, controlled by the rival Federalist Party, took thirty-six ballots to make Jefferson president. Some representatives had thought that Burr would be the lesser of two evils as president. They had to be convinced to vote for Jefferson.

To prevent this from happening again, the Twelfth Amendment was approved in 1804. It required electors to vote separately for the president and vice president. In the absence of a majority of electoral votes, the House of Representatives would choose the president from among the top three candidates. Each state still cast one vote, and the winner had to receive a majority of the votes. Under similar circumstances, the Senate would elect a vice president from the top two candidates. This arrangement continues in operation today. It has been used once to decide on a vice president and twice to elect a president. In the election of 1836, Democratic senator Richard M. Johnson of Kentucky was Martin Van Buren's choice for vice president. He received one electoral vote less than the majority needed to win. The Senate chose him by a vote of 33 to 16.

In 1824, there were four presidential candidates, all members of the Democratic Party. Andrew Jackson received 43.1 percent of the popular vote but only ninety-nine electoral votes. His closest competitor, John Quincy Adams, won 30.9 percent of the popular vote and eighty-four electoral votes. Jackson had failed to get a majority of the electoral votes needed to become president. The election was thrown into the House of Representatives, which chose John Quincy Adams. One of the other candidates, Henry Clay, had encouraged his supporters to vote for Adams. Andrew Jackson was furious, but the election was valid.

In 1876, the House of Representatives had to choose between Democrat Samuel J. Tilden and Republican Rutherford B. Hayes. In a very close election, each party had claimed the electoral votes in Florida, Louisiana, and South Carolina. Both the Republicans and the Democrats were guilty of improper election activities in the three states. They had used bribery and violence to affect the voter turnout. The House of Representatives had to set up a special commission to settle the matter. Finally, a political compromise was reached. The disputed votes went to the Republican candidate. In exchange, the South received government funds to rebuild its economy, destroyed by the Civil War. Also, the remaining federal troops occupying the South were withdrawn. Hayes was given 185 electoral votes; Tilden, 184.

Some reformers have suggested a way to keep the House of Representatives from electing a president. If the candidates were tied or failed to get a majority of the electoral vote, a runoff election would be held between the leading competitors. The people would decide the winner. This idea is attractive, but it presents the same problems as plans for the direct election of the president. In addition, since many people don't vote in presidential elections, they might be even more reluctant to take part in a runoff election.

Usually, the process of electing the president is completed when the electoral votes are cast and counted. After the

☆ ═══════ ☆

*President-elect Clinton's victory was made
official as the tally of the electoral votes was announced
in Congress on Wednesday, January 6, 1993.*

November election, the winning candidate's electors meet in
each state on the Monday following the second Wednesday in
December, a date set by federal law. They vote separately for the
president and the vice president. The results are counted on
January 6 in front of the newly elected Congress. Two hundred
seventy votes is the minimum number needed for victory. The
vice president announces the official totals. Vice Presidents
Martin Van Buren in 1836 and George H. W. Bush in 1988 had
the pleasure of reporting their own election as president. Once
this is done, the lengthy process of getting nominated, campaigning, and voting is completed. The nation has chosen
another president.

WHERE THE PRESIDENTS WERE BORN

☆ **Arkansas**
Bill Clinton

☆ **California**
Richard M. Nixon

☆ **Georgia**
Jimmy Carter

☆ **Illinois**
Ronald W. Reagan

☆ **Iowa**
Herbert C. Hoover

☆ **Kentucky**
Abraham Lincoln

☆ **Massachusetts**
John Adams
John Quincy Adams
John F. Kennedy
George H. W. Bush

☆ **Missouri**
Harry S. Truman

☆ **Nebraska**
Gerald R. Ford

☆ **New Hampshire**
Franklin Pierce

☆ **New Jersey**
Grover Cleveland

☆ **New York**
Martin Van Buren
Millard Fillmore
Theodore Roosevelt
Franklin D. Roosevelt

☆ **North Carolina**
James K. Polk
Andrew Johnson

☆ **Ohio**
Rutherford B. Hayes
James A. Garfield
Benjamin Harrison
William McKinley
William H. Taft
Warren G. Harding
Ulysses S. Grant

☆ **Pennsylvania**
James Buchanan

☆ **South Carolina**
Andrew Jackson

☆ **Texas**
Dwight D. Eisenhower
Lyndon B. Johnson

☆ **Vermont**
Chester A. Arthur
Calvin Coolidge

☆ **Virginia**
George Washington
Thomas Jefferson
James Madison
James Monroe
William H. Harrison
John Tyler
Zachary Taylor
Woodrow Wilson

GOVERNORS WHO BECAME PRESIDENT

☆

Thomas Jefferson ☆ Virginia

Martin Van Buren ☆ New York

William H. Harrison ☆ Indiana Territory

John Tyler ☆ Virginia

James K. Polk ☆ Tennessee

Andrew Johnson ☆ Tennessee

Rutherford B. Hayes ☆ Ohio

Grover Cleveland ☆ New York

William McKinley ☆ Ohio

Theodore Roosevelt ☆ New York

Woodrow Wilson ☆ New Jersey

Calvin Coolidge ☆ Massachusetts

Franklin D. Roosevelt ☆ New York

Jimmy Carter ☆ Georgia

Ronald W. Reagan ☆ California

Bill Clinton ☆ Arkansas

LAWMAKERS WHO BECAME PRESIDENT

Members of the House of Representatives

James Madison

Andrew Jackson

William H. Harrison

John Tyler

James K. Polk

Millard Fillmore

Franklin Pierce

James Buchanan

Abraham Lincoln

Andrew Johnson

Rutherford B. Hayes

James A. Garfield

William McKinley

John F. Kennedy

Lyndon B. Johnson

Richard M. Nixon

Gerald R. Ford

George H. W. Bush

Members of the Senate

James Monroe

John Quincy Adams

Andrew Jackson

Martin Van Buren

John Tyler

Franklin Pierce

James Buchanan

Andrew Johnson

Benjamin Harrison

Warren G. Harding

Harry S. Truman

John F. Kennedy

Lyndon B. Johnson

Richard M. Nixon

MILITARY HEROES WHO BECAME PRESIDENT
☆

George Washington ☆ War of Independence

Andrew Jackson ☆ War of 1812

William H. Harrison ☆ Indian fighter

Zachary Taylor ☆ Mexican War

Ulysses S. Grant ☆ Civil War

Dwight D. Eisenhower ☆ World War II

MAJOR POLITICAL PARTIES IN AMERICAN HISTORY
☆

Name	Presidential Elections
Federalist	1796–1816
Democratic–Republican	1796–1824
Democratic	1828–present
National Republican	1828–1832
Whig	1836–1852
Republican	1856–present

THIRD PARTIES IN AMERICAN HISTORY*

☆

Name	Presidential Candidate	Election Year
Anti-Masonic	William Wirt	1832
Liberty	James G. Birney	1844
Free Soil	Martin Van Buren	1848
	John P. Hale	1852
American (Know-Nothing)	Millard Fillmore	1856
Democratic (for secession)	John C. Breckinridge	1860
Constitutional Union	John Bell	1860
Greenback	James B. Weaver	1880
	Benjamin F. Butler	1884
Prohibition	John P. St. John	1884
	Clinton B. Fisk	1888
	John Bidwell	1892
	John G. Woolley	1900
	Silas C. Swallow	1904
	Eugene W. Chafin	1908
	Eugene W. Chafin	1912
	James Franklin Hanly	1916
People's (Populist)	James B. Weaver	1892
	William Jennings Bryan	1896
	William Jennings Bryan	1900
Socialist	Eugene V. Debs	1900
	Eugene V. Debs	1904
	Eugene V. Debs	1908
	Eugene V. Debs	1912
	Allan Louis Benson	1916
	Eugene V. Debs	1920
	Norman Thomas	1932
Progressive	Theodore Roosevelt	1912
	Robert M. La Follette	1924
	Henry A. Wallace	1948
States' Rights (Dixiecrat)	Strom Thurmond	1948
American Independent	George C. Wallace	1968
National Unity	John B. Anderson	1980
United We Stand	H. Ross Perot	1992

*Candidates listed received 1 percent or more of the popular vote.

absentee ballot a piece of paper listing the candidates for office. It is mailed to voters who are ill or are temporarily absent from their place if they tell state officials in advance that they will be unavailable to vote on Election Day.

amendment a formal change in the Constitution's rules and procedures. For an amendment to be added to the Constitution, two-thirds of the lawmakers in Congress must agree to suggest the change and three-fourths of the states must accept it. There are now twenty-seven amendments to the Constitution.

brokered conventions the result of political party leaders meeting in private to agree on a candidate for president and engineer his nomination by instructing their state delegations to support their choice.

campaigns appeals to the public to vote for a certain candidate or to vote for all the candidates of a certain party.

caucus a meeting of members of Congress from the same political party to choose a candidate for president. Now, a congressional caucus refers to meetings of a party's lawmakers for purposes other than nominating a president. The word also describes gatherings of political party members in voting districts within a state to select a presidential candidate. For example, Iowa is a state that has a caucus system of nomination.

coattails effect occurs when a popular presidential nominee helps other members of the party win national, state, or local offices.

Congress the nation's lawmakers, who serve either in the House of Representatives for two-year terms or in the Senate for six-year terms. The number of representatives elected from each state depends on the size of its population. Each state has two senators.

Constitution   a written document describing and limiting the powers of the national government. It went into effect in 1789.

dark horse   a candidate whose name is unfamiliar to the public.

delegates   individuals who represent the party members in their states at political conventions.

Electoral College   refers to the presidential electors from all the states.

electoral votes   official votes cast by electors from each state to choose the president of the United States.

electorate   members of the public who can vote.

electors   people chosen in each state to cast the state's electoral votes for president.

exit polls   surveys that ask people how they have voted as they leave their voting places on Election Day. From these polls, a winner can be predicted.

favorite son   governors or other state officials presented by state delegations as their candidates for president at party conventions, even though these candidates do not have enough support outside their states to win the party's nomination. Becoming a favorite son was an honor or reward for outstanding public service. It could also be used as a method of withholding a state's delegate votes to trade them for political favors at the party convention.

focus groups   individuals selected for certain qualities, such as age or income, who talk together about particular topics with a discussion leader.

inauguration the ceremony that officially installs the president in office.

keynote address a speech at a national convention that whips up enthusiasm.

landslide elections contests in which the winning candidate receives a very large percentage of the popular vote.

national party conventions large-scale gatherings of delegates representing party members from each state, which meet every four years to choose a presidential candidate.

negative campaigning releasing and emphasizing unflattering or potentially damaging information about the other party's candidate.

off-year elections years when presidential elections are not held.

party platform statement of the party's stand on the political issues of the day.

political action committees independent organizations that take stands on issues, contribute money to candidates, and rally support for them but are not connected with a political party.

political parties organizations that sponsor candidates for public office and help them get elected.

polls surveys that question people about their opinions of the candidates and issues.

primaries elections to choose the party's candidates for public office.

runoff election held between the leading candidates of a previous election when there is a tie or no one has received a majority of the vote.

secret ballot a guarantee of privacy for voters so that no one knows whom they chose unless the voters decide to reveal their selections.

super delegates delegate positions reserved for elected and party officials at Democratic National Conventions.

third party a minor political party that polls over 1 percent of the vote in a presidential election but lacks enough supporters nationwide for its candidate to win.

unit rule a requirement at Democratic national conventions until 1968 that state delegations cast all their votes for the candidate favored by a majority of the state's delegates.

SOURCES USED

Boller, Paul F., Jr. *Presidential Campaigns.* New York: Oxford University Press, 1985.

De Gregorio, William A. *The Complete Book of U.S. Presidents.* New York: Barricade Books, 1993.

Euchner, Charles C., and John Anthony Maltese. *Selecting the President: From Washington to Bush.* Washington, D.C.: Congressional Quarterly Press, 1992.

Federal Election Commission. *1991–1992 Campaign Summary Reports for Clinton, Bush.* 13 January 1994.

———. *The Presidential Public Funding Program.* April 1993.

———. "Ninety–two Presidential Candidates Report Raising $21 Million in 1991." Press release, 19 February 1992.

Freidel, Frank. *Our Country's Presidents.* Washington, D.C.: National Geographic Society, 1966.

League of Women Voters. *Who Will Elect the President? The Electoral College System.* Washington, D.C.: League of Women Voters Education Fund, 1980.

Milkis, Sidney, and Michael Nelson. *The American Presidency: Origins and Development, 1776–1990.* Washington, D.C.: Congressional Quarterly Press, 1990.

Rohter, Larry. "Florida Is Rethinking the Way Presidents Are Elected." *New York Times,* 7 June 1992, sec. 1. *Time,* 1992, passim.

U.S. Department of Commerce, Bureau of the Census. *Statistical Abstract of the United States 1991.* Washington, D.C.: United States Government Printing Office, 1991.

White, Theodore. *America in Search of Itself: The Making of the President 1956–1980.* New York: Harper & Row, 1982.

———. *Breach of Faith: The Fall of Richard Nixon.* New York: Atheneum, 1975.

———. *The Making of the President 1960.* New York: Pocket Books, 1961.

World Almanac and Book of Facts 1994. New York: Funk & Wagnalls, 1993.

☆ ═══════ FURTHER READING ═══════ ☆

Archer, Jules. *Winners and Losers: How Elections Work in America.* San Diego: Harcourt Brace Jovanovich Junior Books, 1984.

Feinberg, Barbara Silberdick. *American Political Scandals: Past and Present.* New York: Franklin Watts, 1992.

Hargrove, Jim. *The Story of Presidential Elections.* New York: PLB/Harper and Row, 1988.

Hewett, Joan. *Getting Elected: The Diary of a Campaign.* New York: Dutton, 1989.

Priestly, E. J. *Finding Out about Elections.* North Pomfret, Vt.: Trafalgar Press, 1983.

Raber, Thomas R. *Presidential Campaigns.* Minneapolis: Lerner, 1988.

Reische, Diana. *Electing a U.S. President.* New York: Franklin Watts, 1992.

Sullivan, George. *Campaigns and Elections.* Morristown, N.J.: Silver Burdett, 1991.

☆ ═══ ABOUT THE AUTHOR ═══ ☆

Barbara Silberdick Feinberg graduated with honors from Wellesley College where she was elected to Phi Beta Kappa. She holds a Ph.D. in political science from Yale University. Among her more recent books are *Watergate: Scandal in the White House, American Political Scandals Past and Present, The National Government, State Governments, Local Governments, Words in the News: A Student's Dictionary of American Government and Politics, Harry S. Truman, John Marshall: The Great Chief Justice, Hiroshima and Nagasaki,* and *Black Tuesday: The Stock Market Crash of 1929.* She has also written *Marx and Marxism, The Constitution: Yesterday, Today, and Tomorrow,* and *Franklin D. Roosevelt, Gallant President.* She is a contributor to *The Young Reader's Companion to American History.*

Mrs. Feinberg lives in New York City with her sons Jeremy and Douglas and two Yorkshire terriers, Katie and Holly. Among her hobbies are growing African violets, collecting antique autographs of historical personalities, and listening to the popular music of the 1920s and 1930s.